THE DAY I SAID GOODBYE AND HELLO

A STORY ABOUT BIG FEELINGS IN A LITTLE BUNNY'S HEART

By: Dr. Luis Leon AMFT
Illustrated by Moch F. Shobaru

Published by : Lumen Leonis Publishing

No parts of this book may be reproduced,
scanned, stored, or transmitted in any form
by any means without written permission.

Please preserve the author's rights and purchase only authorized editions.

Copyright © 2025
All Rights Reserved.

Acknowledgement:

This story was inspired by the "Seven Core Issues of Adoption" framework by Sharon Kaplan Roszia and Deborah Silverstein. We honor their work inhelping professionals and families better understand the emotional landscape of the adoption process. This work uses the framework as a conceptual reference; all characters and stories are original and developed independently.

Once there was a little bunny named Benny who had two homes in his heart.

One day, Benny had to say goodbye to the home where he was born.

He didn't understand why.
He only knew that something
was ending.

He packed his tiny things: His leaf blanket, his pebble collection, and a drawing of his birth mama.

Benny cried quiet tears in the dark and whispered, "Goodbye."

A new family of rabbits welcomed him with open paws.

They had warm soup and silly songs.
But everything still felt different.

"I miss my old home," Benny whispered.

"You're allowed to miss it," said Mama Rabbit, wrapping him in a soft hug.

"You can carry more than
one home in your heart.
And more than one family too."

Some days, Benny was happy.

Other days, he felt lost.

Sometimes both feelings came at once.

"It's okay to feel everything," said Papa Rabbit.
"All your feelings belong here."

Benny started drawing his old home and his new one.

He made a memory box with things from both.

Each time he opened it,
he whispered, "Hello again."

One morning, Benny hopped through the garden and felt the breeze.

"I still miss my first home," he said.
"But now I have another one, too."

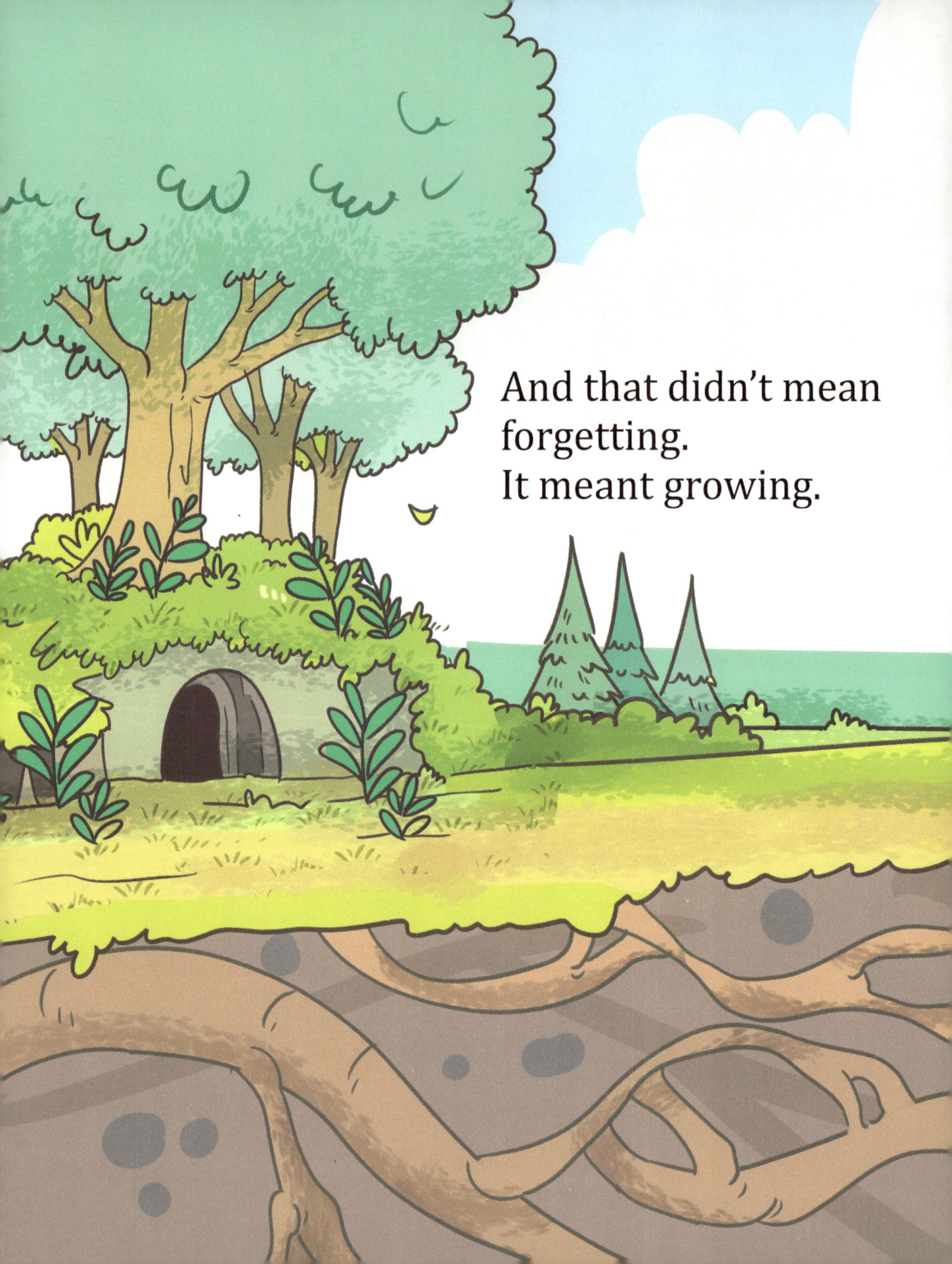

Benny had said goodbye.
And now, he could say hello.

Let's Talk About It

- What are some things you've said goodbye to?
- What's something new you've said hello to?
- What memories would you put in your own memory box?

Notes for Grown-Ups
This story helps children process loss as a central part of adoption. It normalizes mixed feelings and introduces symbolic tools (like a memory box or drawing) for grief expression.

About the Author

Dr. Leon first became interested in mental health while serving in the United States Army. During his time in service, he observed how fellow soldiers could greatly benefit from accessible, compassionate mental health support. This realization led him to change his academic path to psychology.

After completing his military service, he earned a Master's degree in Clinical Psychology with an emphasis in Marriage and Family Therapy from Pepperdine University. While originally planning to work with adult and veteran populations, an unexpected opportunity during his practicum allowed him to work with school-aged children in need of a positive male role model. He embraced the role and discovered a deep passion for helping young people.

Following graduation, he continued working with both children and adults. Over time, he was drawn to supporting children and families navigating the complexities of adoption. He sought out specialized training to become an adoption competent therapist and has since worked with clients across both pre- and post-adoption journeys.

Committed to understanding how systems influence behavior and policy, he also pursued a Ph.D. in Psychology, Public Policy, and Law with an emphasis is in Criminal Behavior from Alliant International University. His work bridges clinical practice, advocacy, and education, while bringing heart, science, and structure to every story he helps shape.

www.ingramcontent.com/pod-product-compliance
Lightning Source LLC
LaVergne TN
LVHW072054070426
835508LV00002B/86